ARON RALSTON
Pinned in a Canyon

BY ROBERTA BAXTER

Published by The Child's World®
1980 Lookout Drive • Mankato, MN 56003-1705
800-599-READ • www.childsworld.com

Acknowledgments
The Child's World®: Mary Berendes, Publishing Director
Red Line Editorial: Design, editorial direction, and production
Photographs ©: Richard Hartog/AP Images, cover, 1; Shutterstock Images, 4; Lee
Cohen/Corbis, 6; Nora Feller/Corbis, 8; Steve Krull/iStockphoto, 10; Nick Rains/
Corbis, 12; iStockphoto, 14; Mickey Krakowski/AP Images, 16; Gary Caskey/Reuters/
Newscom, 18; Joe Scarnici/Getty Images, 20

ISBN 9781634074698

LCCN 2015946301

Printed in the United States of America
Mankato, MN
December, 2015
PA02286

ABOUT THE AUTHOR

Roberta Baxter has lived in the western United States for most of her life. She
enjoys hiking and camping. Her writing includes more than 25 books about
science and history for students of all ages.

TABLE OF
CONTENTS

Chapter 1

Trapped! 4

Chapter 2

How Did He Get Here? 8

Chapter 3

Counting the Hours 12

Chapter 4

I Have to Do This 16

Chapter 5

Still the Outdoorsman 18

Glossary 22
Source Notes 23
To Learn More 24
Index 24

TRAPPED!

April 26, 2003 was a fine day eastern Utah. There was blue sky above and red rocks and juniper trees all around. Aron Ralston planned to bike 15 miles (24.1 km) through Horseshoe Canyon. When he was done, he would leave his bike and hike another 15 miles through Blue John Canyon. There, Ralston would arrive back at his truck and drive to pick up his bike. The entire trip would take a day.

Ralston carried a 25-pound (11.3 kg) backpack with supplies. Inside the backpack was a gallon of water in a **hydration system**, plus another liter of water in a bottle. He also packed two burritos, a muffin, and five chocolate bars. The heaviest part of his load was his climbing gear. That included **carabiners**, webbing, ropes, a **multi-tool** with knife blades and a file, and a headlamp. He also carried his CD player, CDs, extra batteries, a digital video camera, and a camera.

This day was not unusual for Ralston. The day before, he had taken a four-hour bike ride. The day before that, he and a friend had climbed and skied Mount Sopris in western Colorado. Ralston loved to spend time outdoors.

After riding for 15 miles, he locked his bike to a tree and began to hike. As Ralston followed the trail in Blue John Canyon, he met two hikers and introduced himself. They tried to convince him to hike with them. But Ralston wanted to see **petroglyphs** in the canyon, so he went off in a different direction alone. This would prove to be a decision that would change his life forever.

Ralston entered a narrow **slot canyon**, which was mostly only 18 inches (45.7 cm) wide. Large boulders blocked passage in some sections through the canyon. A few he had to crawl under,

and others he scrambled over. Ralston stood on a ledge in the canyon wall. He saw that his next obstacle was a boulder about the size of a truck tire. He shoved it with his foot to see if it was stable. It seemed to be. Ralston turned to slide down the front of the boulder. Suddenly, he felt the boulder shift from his weight. He immediately dropped about 9 feet (2.7 m) to the canyon floor. But the boulder didn't stop moving. It started rolling toward him. Ralston couldn't move backwards without falling off of a ledge. He threw his hands up above his head to push his body away from the rock. But the boulder slammed his left hand against the canyon wall. It then bounced back and smashed into his right hand. The boulder pinned his right hand against the wall.

Ralston tried to tug his hand loose, but it was stuck. Using the strength of his whole body, he tried to shift the boulder enough to release his hand. *"Come on . . . move!"* he thought.[1] Nothing moved. Ralston realized he was trapped with his hand jammed under a boulder. And he was in a tiny canyon, where very few people ever go.

◄ **Many hikers use ropes to navigate through deep slot canyons. Slot canyons are made from water rushing through rock over time.**

Chapter 2

HOW DID HE GET HERE?

Ralston's family moved from Indiana to Colorado when he was 12. Before that time, he had never been more than 10 miles (16.1 km) west of the Mississippi River. Colorado and the West seemed like a foreign country to him. He thought everyone just rode horses and skied all the time.

Ralston tried skiing once he was in Colorado, and he enjoyed it. In the summer, he traveled into the backcountry of Rocky Mountain National Park with a camping group. He was entranced by the experience. Ralston climbed his first fourteener, Longs Peak, in 1994.

Ralston returned to the east for college at Carnegie Mellon University in Pittsburgh, Pennsylvania. He earned a bachelor's degree in mechanical engineering. After college, he accepted an engineering job in Arizona.

After five years, he left his job to allow more time for outdoor activities. He moved to Aspen, Colorado, and worked in an outdoors equipment shop. He wanted to climb all of Colorado's fourteeners in the wintertime alone. It was a something that

COLORADO'S FOURTEENERS

Fourteeners are mountains that are more than 14,000 feet (4,267.2 m) tall. Colorado has more than any other state—53 in all. Some are famous, such as Pikes Peak at 14,115 feet (4,302.3 m) and Longs Peak at 14,255 feet (4,344.9 m). The tallest in Colorado is Mount Elbert, 14,433 feet (4,399.2 m).

▲ Pikes Peak was the inspiration for the poem and song, "America the Beautiful."

had never been done. By April 2003, he had climbed 45 of the 53 fourteeners.

Ralston had faced danger just a month before he became trapped in the canyon. He and two friends were skiing when they were hit by an **avalanche**. One friend was caught in the snow by his feet. Ralston was tossed around by the avalanche. Once Ralston had stopped, his whole body except for his head was buried in the snow. His friend dug him out. Then they found and rescued their second friend, who was completely buried.

Now he faced danger alone in Blue John Canyon. Ralston pulled out his multi-tool. He tried to use the knife blade and the file to chip away at the boulder. His left hand was scratched and sore, but could still lift things. Ralston hoped to remove enough of the rock so that he could pull his hand out and escape.

Ralston knew that he had broken the number one rule of climbing. He had not left a detailed trip plan with anyone. On other trips, he would leave a list of trails or canyons with a roommate or a park ranger. Not this time. His roommates only knew that he would be somewhere near Moab, Utah.

He had gone to Blue John Canyon on an impulse, and now he was trapped. No one would know where to look for him. He knew he had blown it this time.

Chapter 3

COUNTING THE HOURS

After an hour or so of work, Ralston realized that the rock that had fallen on his hand was too hard. He was making little progress chipping away at it. Eventually, he used another rock to pound on the boulder near his hand. But it still didn't move. If the boulder had been softer, he might have been able to scrape enough off to get his hand out. Ralston knew that his hand was damaged enough that it could probably not be saved, even by doctors.

The temperature was comfortable, around 55 degrees Fahrenheit (12 °C) during the day. Ralston's biggest problem was lack of water. His hydration system was empty. He only had 22 ounces (650.6 mL) left in his drinking bottle. Ralston began to take only sips of water every 90 minutes. He stretched it out longer if he could stand it. He remembered a survivor's trick and saved his urine in his empty hydration system to drink later if necessary.

Standing against the canyon wall with his hand trapped did not allow Ralston to sit. Late in the evening, he fashioned a seat from his ropes and carabiners to get some rest. The next day, he also rigged a system with his ropes to try to shift the boulder, but it didn't work.

As the danger of his situation finally sunk in, Ralston said out loud, "You're gonna have to cut your arm off."[2] But he knew that he wouldn't be able to cut through the bone with his dull knife. Instead, he forced his exhausted left hand to raise the multi-tool and chip away more at the rock.

▲ **Some slot canyon walls can be so close together that sunlight barely reaches the bottom of the canyon.**

At night, the temperatures dropped. Ralston used his backpack to provide some padding between his shoulder and the cold canyon wall. He positioned his camera bag and a grocery sack over his arms. He wrapped his legs in his rope to provide a little protection from the cold. Still, he shivered at night and got little sleep.

The canyon was so narrow that little sun entered. Occasionally, Ralston stretched his legs to their limit just to feel some sun hit them. He videotaped messages each day to explain what had happened and to tell his family that he loved them.

By day four, Ralston was out of water. He knew it was only a matter of time before he would die. Ralston considered cutting his hand. But he couldn't see how he would cut through the bones. He only had the multi-tool, which had become duller by chipping at the rock.

On day five, he sipped on the urine he had saved. It wasn't as bad as he had thought it would be. But Ralston knew he would die of thirst if he couldn't free himself. He scratched his name on the rock above his trapped hand. He wrote the year he was born and April 2003. That was when he thought he would die.

Chapter 4

I HAVE TO DO THIS

By day six, Ralston's thoughts were scrambled. He knew he couldn't survive much longer. He would die without water. Suddenly, he realized that he could break his arm so he wouldn't have to cut the bone. He knew that the hand could not be saved even if rescuers came. It had not had blood flow for six days because of the weight of the rock.

Ralston slammed his arm up and down to break it. Both bones in his arm finally snapped. Using the knife from his multi-tool, he cut through the skin, muscle, and tendon just above his wrist to free himself from the boulder. He later said, "When I amputated, I felt every bit of it. It hurt to break the bone, and it certainly hurt to cut the nerve. But cutting the muscle was not as bad."[3]

When he had finished the cut, he heard a voice in his head say, "*I AM FREE!*"[4]

It was 11:34 a.m. on May 1, 2003. Ralston was surprised to see little bleeding, probably because he was so dehydrated. He wrapped his arm in the grocery bag and used the hydration bag like a sling. He scrambled out of the slot canyon. Only a steep incline blocked him from Blue John Canyon. With his ropes and carabiners, he awkwardly **rappelled** down 60 feet (18.3 m). He landed on the floor of Blue John Canyon. He found water in a small puddle and drank. Ralston still had 8 miles to go to reach his truck.

He walked on and met hikers from Holland who gave him clean water and Oreo cookies. At 3:00 p.m., a helicopter arrived to take him to the hospital. They had been searching for him nearby and were summoned by the hikers.

Chapter 5

STILL THE OUTDOORSMAN

Friends, family, and Ralston's boss had contacted officials after he didn't turn up for work. Search and Rescue teams and park rangers had been looking for him. They found his truck and had been searching the surrounding area. The rescue helicopter flew him to the hospital in Moab, Utah, arriving in 12 minutes. He was able to walk in the door and tell the medical people what had happened.

◄ Ralston, with his parents by his side, spoke at a press conference a week after his rescue.

Later he was flown to the hospital in Grand Junction, Colorado. His mother and father arrived, glad to see him alive.

After several surgeries on his arm, Ralston was fitted with a **prosthetic** hand. He chose to have attachments that would allow him to continue his outdoor adventures. He said in an interview, "My prosthetic is the key. The part replacing my hand includes a climbing pick manufactured by Trango. I plug the device into my arm and use it for both vertical ice and rock. Then I just switch it out for a claw attachment for belaying and rope management."[5]

In the year after his accident, Ralston climbed two fourteeners alone in the winter. He continued his plan to climb them all. Ralston now works as a motivational speaker.

PROSTHETICS

When a person loses a body part from an accident or a disease, prosthetics replace what that body part would do. A prosthetic hand is moved by tiny motors. Muscles in the person's arm send out electrical signals that tell the prosthetic to move.

In 2010, the movie *127 Hours* dramatized Ralston's story. His role was played by actor James Franco.

Ralston had survived six days trapped in the canyon and had managed to escape. His attitude is summed up by Ranger Stephen Swanke, who led the search. "I've been doing search and rescue for 23 years, and I've never seen anything like this. He was just a phenomenal individual with an unbelievable will to live."[6]

◄ **Ralston at the 2010 Toronto International Film Festival seven years after his accident**

GLOSSARY

avalanche (AV-uh-lanch): An avalanche is a rapid push of snow or mud down a mountain. The avalanche roared down the mountain and covered Ralston in a big load of snow.

carabiners (kar-uh-BEE-ners): Carabiners are D-shaped rings that have an opening gate, allowing them to be attached to ropes. Ralston hooked the carabiners to his ropes.

hydration system (hahy-DREY-shun SYS-tuhm): A hydration system is made up of a container in a backpack that holds water and a tube that attaches on the shoulder, so a person can easily take a sip of water. Ralston sipped water from the hydration system to stay alive.

multi-tool (MUHL-tee tool): A multi-tool combines several tools, such as a knife, a file, and a pair of scissors in one case. Ralston had to use the knife from the multi-tool to cut his arm off.

petroglyphs (PE-truh-glifs): Petroglyphs are pictures painted on rock faces by prehistoric people. Ralston wanted to see the petroglyphs in Blue John Canyon.

prosthetic (pros-THET-tik): A prosthetic is a mechanical device that replaces a missing body part. The prosthetic on Ralston's hand allowed him to climb again.

rappelled (ra-PELD): To have rappelled means to have descended a slope using ropes and a device that slows the climber down so he or she won't go too fast. Ralston rappelled down the canyon wall with only one arm.

slot canyon (slot KAN-yuhn): A slot canyon is a narrow valley of rock. Ralston entered a slot canyon.

SOURCE NOTES

1. Aron Ralston. *Between a Rock and a Hard Place.* New York: Atria Books, 2004. Print. 21–24.

2. Ibid. 57.

3. Michael Benoist. "Climber Who Cut Off Hand Looks Back." *National Geographic.* National Geographic Society, 30 Aug. 2004. Web. 7 Jul. 2015.

4. Ralston. 299.

5. Michael Benoist. 30 Aug. 2004.

6. J. Michael Kennedy and Stephanie Simon. "Aron Ralston—The Real Story." *Los Angeles Times.* LA Times, 7 Nov. 2010. Web. 7 Jul. 2015.

TO LEARN MORE

Books

Champion, Neil. *Camping and Hiking.* East Sussex, UK: Wayland Ltd., 2014.

Dugan, Christine. *Defying Gravity! Rock Climbing.* Huntington Beach, CA: Teacher Created Materials, 2012.

Green, Sara. *Hiking.* Minneapolis, MN: Bellwether Media, 2012.

Long, Denise. *Survivor Kid: A Practical Guide to Wilderness Survival.* Chicago, IL: Chicago Review Press, 2011.

Web Sites

Visit our Web site for links about Aron Ralston: childsworld.com/links

Note to Parents, Teachers, and Librarians: we routinely verify our Web links to make sure they are safe and active sites. So encourage your readers to check them out!

INDEX

Blue John Canyon, 4, 5, 11, 17

canyon, 5, 7, 10, 11, 13, 14, 15, 21

Colorado, 5, 8–9
Aspen, 9
Grand Junction, 19

Horseshoe Canyon, 4, 5

Longs Peak, 9

Mount Elbert, 9

Mount Sopris, 5

Rocky Mountain National Park, 9

Pikes Peak, 9

slot canyon, 5, 7, 14, 17

Swanke, Stephen, 21

Utah, 4
Moab, 11, 18